VIKINGS

A Guide to the Terrifying Conquerors

by Sean McCollum

History's Greatest Warriors

Velocity is published by Capstone Press,
151 Good Counsel Drive, P.O. Box 669, Mankato, Minnesota 56002.
www.capstonepub.com

Books published by Capstone Press are manufactured with paper
containing at least 10 percent post-consumer waste.

Library of Congress Cataloging-in-Publication Data
McCollum, Sean.
  Vikings: a guide to the terrifying conquerors/by Sean McCollum.
     p. cm.—(Velocity. History's greatest warriors)
  Includes bibliographical references and index.
  Summary: "Describes Viking warriors, including their training, fighting methods,
and weapons, as well as their decline and their place in popular culture"—Provided
by publisher.
  ISBN 978-1-4296-6603-9 (library binding)
  1. Vikings—Juvenile literature. I. Title. II. Series.
  DL66.M37 2012
  948'.022—dc22   2011000165

Editorial Credits: Russell Primm
Art Director: Suzan Kadribasic
Designers: Divij Singh, Manish Kumar

Photo Credits
Alamy: Tony Cunningham, 1, 28-29, Qrt, 6-7, Danita Delimont, 7, The Art Gallery
Collection, 12 (top), Niels Quist, 13 (top), North Wind Picture Archives, 18-19, 41,
INTERFOTO, 20 (bottom), Stephen Roberts Photography, 22-23, Stephen Giardina,
24-25, OJPHOTOS, 32-33, 19th era, 35, Andia, 38-39, PCN Photography, 45 (bottom);
Bridgeman Art Library: © Look and Learn, 26-27; Corbis: National Geographic Society,
10-11, Bettmann, 43; Dreamstime: Stasys Eidiejus, 9; Getty Images: Hulton Archive, 33
(front); Istockphoto: Duncan Walker, cover, Manuel Velasco, 14 (front); NASA: 45 (top);
Shutterstock: Darren Turner, 5, Freddy Eliasson, 12 (bottom), Algol, 16-17, 3drenderings,
20 (top), 21 (right), AridOcean, 30-31, Charobnica, 36-37; Wikipedia: Carl Larsson &
Gunnar Forssell, 42.

Printed in the United States of America in Melrose Park, Illinois.
032011   006112LKF11

Table of Contents

Sudden Fury from the Sea

The monks must have been stunned by what came ashore that day. Longships approached, oars flashing. They came in fast and slid to a stop in the shallows. Shouting men jumped into the surf carrying swords and axes. A writer later described them as a group of "stinging hornets."

Their target was the abbey on Lindisfarne, a small island near England's coast. The church of St. Cuthbert was there. It was a peaceful place of learning. It was also a storehouse of church treasures. The monks prayed, tended their gardens, and copied pages of the Bible at the abbey. They had little reason to be on guard. The fierce North Sea had kept the place safe from attack for 150 years—until now.

Exactly what happened on June 8, 793, is lost. The raiders probably plundered the barns and workshops, then set them on fire. They battered their way into the church and living quarters. They ripped down tapestries. They pried out whatever precious stones caught their eyes. Holy crucifixes and candlesticks were stolen.

Some of the monks escaped. Others were hacked to death. Yet others were driven into the sea and drowned. Some were caught and enslaved in far-off lands.

The raiders loaded their plunder and sailed back out to sea. They disappeared across the water as quickly as they had come.

The attack at Lindisfarne was the first major raid by a new seagoing menace. The age of the Vikings had begun. These fearsome warriors terrorized the shores and waterways of England and Europe for more than 250 years.

4   abbey—a place where monks live and work

Everything we know about Viking raids in Europe was written by the monks—the victims of the attacks! The view they give of the Vikings is very one-sided. **Archaeologists** and historians are working to uncover the rest of the story. They want to learn about the raids from the Vikings' point of view.

The abbey at Lindisfarne was founded by St. Aidan in 635.

archaeologist—someone who uses ancient buildings and artifacts to learn about the past

Vikings: How Do We Know What We Know?

Video cameras and photography didn't exist during the Viking Age, of course. Vikings told their stories orally instead of writing them down. They sometimes carved their adventures in wood or stone. They didn't, however, draw or paint. So how do we know about Vikings and their adventures? Over the centuries, historians looked for clues and did research to piece together their story.

a Viking grave

Archaeology

To learn about the past, archaeologists study historical **artifacts**. These items give them clues about the lives of people who lived long ago. For example, researchers found many silver coins with Arabic markings in Birka. Birka was a Swedish port near where Stockholm is today. This discovery is proof that trade routes connected Viking merchants to Arab traders thousands of miles away. Archaeologists continue to find Viking swords, spears, and arrowheads, too. These tell us about the weapons Vikings used in battle. By studying human skeletons, researchers can figure out how old people were when they died. They can sometimes tell what killed them, too.

Historical Accounts

Monks and priests wrote down accounts of Viking raids. Some of these histories survived and detail the attacks. Viking storytellers also created poems about the adventures of great Viking warriors and kings. These stories hint at what happened and when. Historians know, however, that these accounts are not always reliable. Victims might have exaggerated the power and cruelty of the Vikings. Or Viking warriors might have overstated their cunning and courage to impress their friends and family.

Working Replicas

In the last 100 years, historians have found several buried Viking ships. These offer details about how Viking vessels were built. People have built exact replicas of Viking ships using techniques from the Viking era. The replica ships have been tested at sea. By experiencing how these ships work, researchers learn about Viking technology.

a Viking helmet

artifact—an object made by humans

CHAPTER 1

Who Were the Vikings?

Scandinavia is a region in far northern Europe. Today it includes the countries of Denmark, Norway, and Sweden. These were the homelands of the **Norse**. The name *Viking* was more of a job description, like *pirate* or *raider*. Later, it was used to identify the Scandinavians in general. The first Vikings, though, were not a unified army with a central leader. They were more like gangs that went hunting for treasures to steal.

SCANDINAVIA

Most early Scandinavian communities were along the coasts of Denmark and southern Norway, the coasts and lake districts of Sweden, and the islands of the Baltic Sea. Early settlements were not countries as we think of them today. They were small and organized into communities called chiefdoms.

FARMERS AND SAILORS

Most Norse were farmers. They raised crops and livestock on land around small villages. They were also a coastal people. The waters were both a source of food and a means of transportation. Fishing and sailing helped them become master boat builders and bold sailors.

HUNGRY FOR LAND?

In the 700s, historians think too many people might have lived on too little land in Scandinavia. This might have forced some to sail elsewhere in search of farmland. Landless men might have begun raiding to improve their fortunes. Chieftains assembled warrior groups, called *lids*. These small armies probably started out raiding Scandinavian neighbors. They later cast their eyes across the North Sea.

FACT

Danes, Norwegians, and Swedes speak similar languages that allow them to communicate with one another.

Norse—relating to Scandinavia or Scandinavian people

Norway
Sweden
Denmark

Norwegian Sea

Norway

Sweden

Gulf of
Bothnia

North Sea

Denmark

Baltic
Sea

EASY PICKINGS

Seagoing traders visited far-flung villages to do business. They noticed that many of the places they visited were not well protected. Armed with this information—and axes and swords—Viking bands launched their raids. The more loot these warriors hauled home, the easier it became to get others to join in the raids.

Norse Society

Norse society was made up of three social classes.
Each group had different rights, responsibilities, and freedoms.

NOBLES

Power in Viking culture came from the control of land and men.
The Viking ruling class of nobles included wealthy landholders, chieftains, and some warriors. They managed large tracts of land worked by slaves and tenant farmers. Nobles often kept small private armies and staged independent raids. They also collected **tributes** from those they protected. In turn, the nobles swore loyalty and paid tribute to a more powerful chieftain or king. Nobles also supplied warriors, ships, and service to leaders planning big raids.

FREEMEN

Most people in Viking society were freemen. This class included farmers, merchants, and **artisans**. Farming on small plots was the most common occupation. Artisans, such as cart makers and boat builders, were valued for their skills. Sometimes men of this class put down their tools and took up weapons to join a raiding party. Freemen also had the potential—and faced the risk—of moving between classes. For example, a freeman might be forced to become a slave if he committed a crime or failed to pay a debt. But he could also rise to nobility if he gained wealth from raiding or trading, or if he impressed a powerful chieftain.

SLAVES

Slaves were the lowest class. Most of these women and men were captured in Viking raids and forced to work as laborers, or servants. Any children they had were also considered slaves. All slaves were considered property and could be treated and traded like farm animals. But brutality toward a slave was frowned upon. Slaves could not own land or carry weapons. They gained rights by proving their special worth to their masters. In some cases, slaves found ways to buy their own freedom or were freed after a period of loyal service.

tribute—something given as a sign of respect and appreciation
artisan—someone who is skilled at making something

VIKING WOMEN

A Scandinavian woman in the Viking Age could choose her own husband. She could also divorce him if he was cruel or unfaithful. A resourceful wife was very important to running a good home. She took care of the children. For most married women, their work also included cooking, weaving, sewing, and farm chores. Wives were usually left in charge when husbands went raiding. Some women even became successful traders. A few Viking queens also rose to power.

FACT

Rigsthula

Rigsthula is a mythic Viking poem. It tells of a god that travels the countryside disguised as a man named Rig. He visits three different couples. Each couple gives birth to a son—Thrall, Karl, and Jarl. The myth describes how each boy grows up to be the father of his class—slaves, freemen, and nobles.

This painting shows Vikings coming ashore to settle in Newfoundland.

Viking Arts

The Vikings are often portrayed as **barbarians**. Jewelry, carvings, and metalwork found in grave sites show another side of the Vikings.

METALWORK

Gold and silver made beautiful ornaments, but it was iron that made the Vikings a feared people. They dug up iron ore from bogs and marshes. Then they heated it in small furnaces. Blacksmiths then pounded it into nails, hinges, and farm tools. The finest iron was used to forge swords, axes, spearheads, and other weapons. Good blacksmiths were honored in Viking society. They often play important roles in Viking myths and stories.

JEWELRY

Vikings wore jewelry to display and carry their wealth. In the Viking Age, a king or noble gave gifts of gold bracelets to reward his warriors. He might give gifts to poets who wrote about him. Most jewelry was made from bone and bronze. The very rich had jewelry made of silver and gold. Some jewelry was set with glass beads, amber, or other semi-precious stones. Viking women often wore brooches. They were worn on the chest and held cloaks in place. Men and women also wore neck and arm rings.

barbarian—someone who is wild and uncivilized

WOOD AND STONE CARVING

Scandinavian carpenters decorated much of their work with detailed wood carvings. Stories were sometimes chiseled into chairs and doorways. Ferocious animal heads were carved in the fronts of Viking ships. Woodworkers usually used soft pine or harder oak. Irish stone carvers introduced their craft to the Vikings after raiders settled in Ireland in the mid-800s.

This runic stone carving is known as the Jelling stone. It was raised by Harald Bluetooth.

RUNES

The letters of the Viking alphabet are called runes. They include 16 symbols. Runes consist of straight and angled lines with no curves or horizontal lines. They are easy to carve in stone and wood. Vikings believed runes had magical properties. Warriors sometimes etched them onto their weapons as charms.

Viking Religion

Unlike most Europeans at the time, Vikings were not Christians. They were **pagans**. Viking warriors believed that if they died bravely in battle, female warrior angels known as Valkyries would carry them away. They would be taken to Valhalla, a glorious hall of eternal feasting and fighting. This belief heightened their bravery in battle.

VIKING GODS

Odin was the god of battles and the leader of the Norse gods. He could be violent and cruel, but he was also a lover of knowledge. He sacrificed one of his eyes so he might drink from the fountain of wisdom. Two ravens, Huginn and Muminn, sat on his shoulders. They flew above the world and returned to their master to whisper what they learned. Brave warriors who died in battle hoped to feast with Odin in the afterlife.

Thor was one of Odin's sons. He was a favorite god of Scandinavian farmers and sailors. Many Vikings wore pendants of Thor's hammer, called *Mjöllnir*, for good luck. Thor was the god of strength, promises, and weather. Although Thor was incredibly strong and a fierce fighter, he was not very smart.

statue of Thor

pagan—someone who is not a member of the Christian, Jewish, or Muslim religions; a pagan may worship many gods, nature, or their ancestors

Freyja was the goddess of beauty, love, marriage, fertility, and crops. She was also the goddess of witchcraft, war, and death. Many of the gods and other mythical beings wanted to marry her. She could fly in a cloak sewn of falcon feathers. She rode in a chariot drawn by two cats.

Freyr was Freyja's brother. He was the god of fertility, crops, peace, and prosperity. He owned a magic ship that always found its way and could be folded up and carried in a pocket. He also had a sword that could fight by itself. His trusty steed was the boar Gullinbursti whose mane glowed to light his path.

Loki was a trickster god who often played jokes and made trouble. He could also be brave and helpful. For example, he used his trickery to help Thor recover his stolen hammer from the giant Thrymr. Loki was a shape-shifter capable of appearing as a man or a woman. He could also turn into any animal.

DOOM OF THE GODS

According to Norse mythology, the world will be destroyed in a great battle, called Ragnarök. The gods and their favorite human warriors will face off against giants and mythical beasts. Almost everyone will be killed. The earth will be burned and sink into the sea. Yggdrasil, the world tree, will survive. It will shelter a man and woman who will repopulate a renewed Earth.

SAILING THE SEA

Big Viking ships were capable of open-sea travel. They belonged to two main groups:

Merchant ships were known as *knarr*. They were deeper and more stable than other Viking ships. They also had stronger hulls. They were designed to carry many tons of cargo. Traders used these vessels to ship their goods. Colonists used them to carry people and supplies to new lands.

Longships were sleek vessels designed for raiding and war. They were long with a narrow hull. They had shallow **drafts** that let them navigate in shallow water. The biggest longship was more than 100 feet (30 meters) long and could carry more than 100 warriors to battle.

FACT

In Norse, the "styra bord," or rudder, was always on the right. This is probably the source of the modern term "starboard," meaning the right side of a ship.

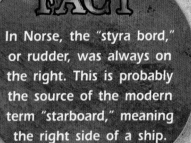

Stern and Bow—Viking ships had a pointed front, or bow, and back, or stern.

Keel—For strength, the keel was cut and shaped from a single length of hard wood. Most shipbuilders used oak.

draft—a measurement of how deep a boat sinks into the water

Hull—The sides of ships were "clinker-built." That means they had overlapping planks held together by iron rivets. This structure made the ship flexible, yet strong. The seams were stuffed with wool, cloth, or plant material, then tarred over to make the hull watertight.

Sail and Mast—A ship's sail was a big square of wool cloth. It provided power on the open sea. Oars were most useful in rivers or shallow waters. The mast could be taken down in the event of a storm or when the ship got close to shore. The ship's men would then use oars to row.

Viking longship

REASONS FOR RAIDING

Historians often choose the raid on Lindisfarne in 793 as the beginning of the Viking Age. Evidence suggests Vikings were already attacking other Norse settlements before then. The big change came when Viking longships crossed the wild North Sea to hit the coasts of Britain and Europe. Several factors probably lured—or forced—Vikings from their homelands during the Viking Age.

Trade

Scandinavian traders ventured to other lands long before Viking warriors began their raids. Evidence shows they were already exchanging goods with people in England and Ireland thousands of years ago. Later, foreign traders began visiting Norse market towns. Trade clearly exposed Scandinavians to the wealth of other lands.

Lief Eriksson was a Viking explorer.

Raid

Scandinavian traders probably returned home and talked about the rich foreign towns they had visited. It is likely that they told their warrior friends how defenseless many of these places were. Once Vikings raiders returned with loot and exciting stories, chances are others wanted to join the raids.

Invade and Explore

Problems in Scandinavia might have sparked Viking raids. Land and income might have been scarce for young people. They may also have just been greedy. Stronger chieftains who wanted more land might have forced others to flee. For some Vikings, these events drove them to invade and settle in other places. This started with Vikings settling in Scotland, England, or even as far south as Normandy in France, by the 800s. Others may have joined expeditions that promised a new start, such as the group that explored and **colonized** Iceland sometime between 871 and 874.

colonize—to settle in a new area

CHAPTER 2

Gear, Weapons, and Tools of the Raid

Viking combat was often a face-to-face, hand-to-hand affair. Young Vikings learned how to use bows, spears, axes, and knives while hunting or doing chores.

AXES

An ax in the hands of a strong-armed Viking was a ferocious weapon. A well-aimed blow could smash through any shield or split an iron helmet. A Viking battle ax had a long chopping edge. The handle, called the haft, could be more than 6 feet (2 m) long.

SWORDS

A double-edged sword was expensive and a sign of high status. It was held with a single hand while the other hand held a shield or another weapon. A blacksmith hammered out a firm but flexible core for the blade of a good sword. Then he welded on steel edges that were strong and sharp.

SEAXES

A seax was a type of single-edged knife. Viking freemen used them for daily chores, but they could also be deadly in hand-to-hand combat. Warriors carried them in horizontal sheaths worn on a belt.

BOWS AND ARROWS

Viking bows were hunting weapons that were also deadly on the battlefield. They were usually carved from yew or elm wood. Arrows were tipped with barbed or leaf-shaped iron arrowheads. Powerful bows have been found in Viking graves. Some could shoot an arrow a distance of more than two football fields!

SPEARS

Spears were common Viking weapons. Their shafts were made from ash wood. Spearheads were forged from iron. Shorter, pointier spearheads were designed for throwing. Longer, wider blades could be used for slashing. Viking spears ranged from 6.5 feet (2 m) to nearly 10 feet (3 m).

spear

BATTLE DRESS

Viking nobles and freemen could join raiding expeditions. Most warriors were expected to provide their own gear and weapons. Rich nobles would carry the best equipment. Poorer peasants, often made do with whatever they could get their hands on.

Peasant Warrior

Head gear—Raiders who could not afford helmets might have worn tough leather caps that offered some protection.

Body armor—Warriors who couldn't afford leather tunics and chain mail might have worn thick tunics of linen or canvas.

Ax—Peasant warriors might have charged into battle with the same axes they used to chop down trees.

Knives—A good sword was out of the price range of most peasants. They probably carried long, single-edged knives.

People dressed as warriors for a Viking reenactment festival in Denmark.

Noble Warrior

Head gear—Warriors wore iron helmets with nose guards. Some helmets also had eye guards.

Body armor—Viking warriors wore padded leather tunics or chain mail. Made of small iron rings, chain mail was heavy yet flexible.

Shield—Whether noble or peasant, most Viking warriors carried shields. Most shields were round and made of wood with leather edges.

Ax—Noble warriors had fine battle axes with long chopping edges.

Sword—Double-edged swords were the favorite weapons of Vikings who could afford them.

DREADED VIKING LONGBOATS

The Viking Age would not have been possible without longboats. The strong, flexible warships withstood rough seas. Their design also let them cruise into shallow water or up rivers. This allowed Viking warriors to land close to their targets. Historians think captains of Viking warships preferred to sail in small groups of three or more ships. Viking kings organized fleets of hundreds of ships for major invasions. Most Viking warships carried 25 to 60 warriors.

Figurehead—Warships belonging to kings and chieftains often had carved dragon heads on the bow. The fierce faces were meant to scare sea monsters and evil spirits. They were also a warning to human enemies.

Shield Rack—Shields hung along the outside of the ship. The design helped protect warriors from arrows and spears in the event of sea battles.

Oars—Viking warships usually had 20 to 30 oarsmen. Sometimes two men would pull on each oar to move the ship faster. Each oar was about 18 feet (5.5 m) long. The ships did not have benches or storage below the deck. The rowers sat on chests that contained their belongings.

Hull—The bottoms of Viking warships— the hulls—were flat so they could maneuver in shallow water. The sides were short so the Vikings could quickly jump out once the ships were close to land.

FACT

Viking kings and queens were sometimes buried in ships. Archaeologists have dug up some of these vessels. They have offered great clues about the skill of Viking shipbuilders.

Military Tactics

RAID AND RUN

"We sailed our ships to any shore that offered the best hope of booty," the Viking story of Arrow-Odd recounts. "We feared no fellow on earth, we were fit, we fought in the battle-fleet."

Longboats gave Viking raiders the advantage of surprise. They could sweep in from the sea and land close to coastal abbeys, villages, or farms. The attackers grabbed anything valuable they found, including people to sell as slaves. Then they loaded their boats and sped away. As a rule, Vikings did not stay for long. They did not want to give local people time to mount a defense.

Summer was the season for Viking raids. Crews usually went raiding after planting crops in the spring. They returned home before the autumn harvest. Rough weather between August and April made crossing the North Sea dangerous.

The pattern of raids changed as the 800s unfolded. It seems the Vikings became less willing to make the voyage home after their attacks. By 841 they had established year-round forts in Ireland. In 851 an English writer mentioned that "the heathen stayed through the winter." Vikings had begun to invade and settle.

Vikings captured men and women from the towns they raided and kept them as slaves.

Vikings on the Battlefield

The fighting that took place during Viking attacks was likely a hacking, slashing, free-for-all. In battles between large groups or armies, Viking warriors fought as a team. Historical accounts hint at some of the tactics Vikings used.

Shieldwall

A line of warriors stood behind a wall of overlapping shields. The shields blunted an opponent's charge. Spearmen standing behind the shieldwall thrust their weapons at the enemy between the shields. Archers in the rear also shot arrows over the wall. Shieldwalls did not move easily. This made them vulnerable to attacks from the sides.

Boar Snout

To attack a shieldwall, opponents might use a tactic called the boar snout or swine array. This was a triangular wedge of warriors. They would charge at the enemy line and try to punch their way through.

GOING BERSERKER

According to Norse legend, the most ferocious Viking warriors were known as berserkers. The name came from the Norse word for *bear*, and legends say berserkers wore bearskin robes into battle. Berserkers would work themselves into a frenzy before battle. They attacked the enemy with incredible fury. No wound or blow seemed to slow them. Snorri Sturluson, a 13th-century Viking poet and historian, described berserkers this way:

[They] rushed forward without armor, were as mad as dogs or wolves, bit their shields, and were as strong as bears or wild oxen."

LEADING THE CHARGE

Viking chieftains and kings were expected to be excellent, fearless warriors. It was their duty to lead men into battle. A leader's position on the battlefield was marked by a banner. The battle might end when he was killed.

Household troops, called *huskarlar*, acted as bodyguards to kings and lords. They were usually the best fighters. They might be positioned in the front lines, or held back to rush to any point in need of extra help. They were expected to win or die fighting.

a reenactment of the 1009 Viking raid on the town of Tiel in the Netherlands

THE VIKINGS MOVE IN

In the mid-800s, groups of Vikings began settling in lands they had only raided before. Viking explorers also discovered an empty island in the North Atlantic. They named it Iceland. During the next 200 years, Viking influence spread across Europe. They reached Asia, North Africa, and even North America. The lands and cultures they mixed with changed the Vikings too.

Greenland—Erik the Red sailed from Iceland and landed on this large, glacier-covered island in 982.

Iceland—After Viking sailors discovered Iceland in 860, settlers followed to establish a colony.

Ireland—By 841 the Vikings had established forts in Ireland. Dublin, today's capital of Ireland, was originally a Viking settlement.

Newfoundland—Leif Eriksson, the son of Erik the Red, explored this island off North America in about the year 1000. Norse settlers lived here for a short time, but they did not succeed in colonizing the island.

England—Viking chieftains began invading England in the 850s. Years of warfare followed.

Paris—Hundreds of Viking ships sailed up the River Seine and laid siege to Paris in 885 and 886. They left when city officials gave them 700 pounds (318 kg) of silver and free passage on the river.

Kiev—Vikings captured the town of Kiev sometime between 858 and 879 and made it the capital of the region.

Normandy—The French king gave Viking chieftain Rollo this land in 911. In return, Rollo promised peace and to defend the area from other Vikings. Normandy means "Northman's Land."

Constantinople—In the early 900s, the Vikings attacked the capital of the Byzantine Empire but failed to capture it.

NATION BUILDING

Vikings did more than just raid and invade. In their homelands kings and chieftains made deals and fought wars to bring more people and territory under their control. The nations of Denmark, Norway, Sweden, and Iceland all took form during the Viking era.

Denmark

The peninsula and islands that became Denmark have always had good soil for farming. The Danes were also in a great location for trading. These features brought wealth and power to the Viking kings and chieftains there. By the early 800s, the Danes had become somewhat united under King Godfred. After his death in 810, civil war broke out. More than 150 years later, the kingdom was unified again under Harald Bluetooth. Harald built a chain of circular fortresses known as the Trelleborg forts.

FACT

Bluetooth technology lets wireless users connect their cell phones and other wireless devices. The company is named after Harald Bluetooth, who united the Danes in the 900s. The company's logo is made from two runes that stand for Harald's initials.

Sweden

Two groups of people, the Svear and Götar, controlled Sweden at the start of the Viking Age. King Olof Skötkonung ruled over both groups from 995 to 1022. The nation was not completely unified until 1172. Today Swedes call their country Sverige, named for the Svear.

Iceland

A sailor named Gardar the Swede is said to have landed on this volcanic island in about 860. It was mainly colonized by Norwegian settlers after that. By 1100 as many as 40,000 people might have lived there. Today much of what people know about the Vikings is taken from the writings of Iceland's poets, known as *skalds*. They wrote many Viking legends, sagas, and histories.

Norway

Norway was made up of several small chiefdoms and kingdoms when the Viking Age began. Some were controlled by the Danes. Harald Fairhair brought most of the country under his rule in the late 800s. Danish and Norwegian kings wrestled for power there for another 150 years. Led by Magnus the Good and the kings that followed, the people of Norway gained self-rule by 1100.

statue of Harald Fairhair

CHAPTER 4

Viking Invasion

THE VIKINGS IN ENGLAND AND NORMANDY

The Vikings moved into parts of England, Ireland, and France after decades of raiding. Their colonization of these areas from 850 to 911 caused big changes for the invaders and the invaded.

England

For a while in the 800s, the **Anglo-Saxons** were able to block Viking attempts to invade England. But fleets from the north kept coming. In 865 a large force of Danish Vikings got a foothold in East Anglia. East Anglia is now part of eastern England. By 876 they had conquered several kingdoms. Viking settlements grew. But the Danes soon blended with the local people, and each side influenced the other. Their territory became known as the Danelaw. English and Viking kings continued to battle for power for the next 190 years.

Normandy

In 885 a large Viking fleet began raiding along the River Seine in northern France. Unable to drive them out, the French king, Charles the Fat, made a deal with the Viking chieftain, Rollo. Rollo and his men could have much of the northern coast if they agreed to three things. They had to be loyal to the French king. They had to defend France against other Viking raiders. And they had to convert to Christianity. Rollo said yes. The region became known as Normandy. In the end it was the French who won over the Vikings. Eventually the descendants of the Viking invaders completely adopted French language and customs.

bICRE
REX

Anglo-Saxon —a person who settled in England in the 400s and 500s

The Norman Conquest

The year 1066 is a landmark in English and European history. That year Harold Godwinson was chosen king of England. Norway's king, Harald Hardrada, invaded and challenged him for the throne. Godwinson won, but the war weakened his forces. Three days after Godwinson's victory, the Normans invaded from across the English Channel. They were led by William, the Duke of Normandy. William defeated and killed Godwinson at the Battle of Hastings. He was crowned king of England and upgraded his title to William the Conqueror. Over the next 20 years he defeated many Danish Viking attempts to overthrow him.

FACT

The Bayeux Tapestry uses thread to tell the tale of William the Conqueror and the Norman Conquest. Pictures of the campaign are embroidered onto cloth. The tapestry is almost 225 feet (69 m) long. That is the length of a 747 jet!

a scene from the Bayeux Tapestry

SIDET: GLORVM STIGANT ARCHI EPS

VIKINGS IN THE EAST

Arab traders and Slavic tribes called them "Rus." They were Vikings, mostly Swedes, who had pushed eastward into what is now Russia. According to history and legend, the Rus became an elite group of merchants and warriors in the region. Their influence stretched from the Baltic Sea to the Caspian and Black seas by the 900s. Over time they blended in with the local tribes, adopting Slavic names and languages.

Kiev—Oleg was a legendary Rus chieftain. He captured the city of Kiev in about 882. It became the capital of the Rus realm. Kiev quickly grew into an important center for politics and trade.

The Dnieper Trade Route—Rus merchants used the Dnieper River as a trade route to and from Constantinople. They often traveled in canoelike dugouts. These boats could navigate narrow waterways. They could also be picked up and carried around rapids and other hazards.

FACT

The rulers of Constantinople were impressed by the Vikings who threatened their great city in the 900s. Many Viking warriors found employment as members of the Varangian Guard. These mercenaries protected the emperor and fought ferociously during his military campaigns.

NORWAY

Oslo

Stoc

NMARK

Copenhage

DS

Berlin

terdam

ERMANY

OURG   Prag

CZEC

IECTENSTEIN

AUST

Ljubljar

SLOVENIA

LY   CRO

SAN
MARINO

Rome   MONT

mercenary —a soldier who is hired to serve in a foreign army

Helsinki

Tallinn
ESTONIA

Staraja Ladoga

Riga
LATVIA

LITHUANIA
Vilnius

RUSSIA

Minsk

BELARUS
Warsaw

AND

Kiev

UKRAINE

Dnieper River

SLOVAKIA
Bratislava
Budapest

MOLDOVA

The Dnieper
Trade Route

UI

b

&

OVIN

ajev

joric

Sofia

Black Sea

Tirana
ALBANIA

Skopje
MACEDONIA

ARIA

Angora

Constantinople

GREESE

TURKEY

RUS

Volga River

The Volga Trade Route

Moscow

Staraja Ladoga—This village became a regional center of Viking trade in the early 800s.

The Volga Trade Route—Rus merchants traveled the Volga River to access Arab goods, especially silver. In exchange, the Rus brought furs, wax, and slaves.

Constantinople—Constantinople is now called Istanbul. It was the capital of the Byzantine Empire. Rus forces attempted to capture it in the early 900s, but failed. Trade with Constantinople gave the Rus access to Chinese silk and other goods from the Far East.

VIKING GREATS

What makes a great leader? For the Vikings it was a combination of bravery, boldness, and victory. In truth, tales of great Vikings are a mix of history and legend. It also didn't hurt to have a great nickname.

Ivar the Boneless was a chieftain who invaded East Anglia, England, in about 865. He became infamous for having King Edmund of East Anglia killed. No one is sure why he was called "the Boneless."

Harald Fairhair is credited with uniting Norway. He supposedly took over the throne at the age of 10. He hoped to bring all Norwegians under his rule. Legend says he vowed not to comb or cut his hair until he succeeded and that is how he got his name. He fulfilled his mission with a major victory at the battle of Hafrsfjord in the late 800s.

Cnut the Great was a powerful Viking king who ruled Denmark, England, Norway, and parts of Sweden in the 1000s. As a teen he joined his father in conquering England in 1013. He claimed the English throne three years later. Remembered as a good king, Cnut made political deals that added to his realm. But his empire broke up quickly after he died in 1035.

a statue of Rollo, a Viking leader who became the first Duke of Normandy

Erik the Red was the founder of the Viking colony on Greenland. In about 983 Erik and his family were forced to leave Iceland. They traveled to Greenland and found good grazing land there. Erik, who had red hair, returned to Iceland and organized a fleet of colonists to settle in Greenland.

Leif Eriksson was the son of Erik the Red. He set out on his own adventure in about 1000. He landed on a northern island of North America, a place he called Vinland. He did not succeed in colonizing it. He returned to Greenland and succeeded his father. Vikings in Greenland continued to visit North America for at least another 80 years.

Olaf Haraldsson was the king of Norway. He championed Christianity in his kingdom. Olaf became a Viking raider at the age of 12. In 1015 he successfully organized a campaign to free Norway from the Danes. While king, he used harsh punishment to force his subjects to accept Christianity. Leading chieftains rebelled and removed him from the throne.

Harald Hardrada is considered one of the last great Viking kings. As a warrior, he fought in Slavic lands before joining the Varangian Guard in Constantinople. In 1047 he became ruler of Norway. He was apparently a ruthless king. His nickname "Hardrada" translates to "hard ruler." In 1066 he invaded England with 300 ships to seize the throne there. He was killed at the Battle of Stamford Bridge.

CHAPTER 5

The Viking Legacy

END OF THE VIKING AGE

The Viking Age lasted for about 250 years. What brought it to an end? The Vikings were not conquered or broken by their enemies. Instead, social changes caused big shifts in the Viking way of life. Scandinavians traded their Viking heritage for national identities. They became Danes, Norwegians, and Swedes. Here are several factors that contributed to the end of the Viking Age.

BETTER DEFENSES

As time passed, victims of Viking raids became better prepared to protect themselves. The **monastery** on the island of Iona is a good example. It moved its community 20 miles (32 km) inland after enduring four Viking attacks in the late 700s and early 800s. Coastal targets were no longer easy pickings, and raiding was no longer an easy way for a Viking to get rich.

BLENDING IN

By the mid-800s, many Vikings were settling in lands they had once raided. They married and had children among local people in Ireland, England, Normandy, and elsewhere. In most cases the children and grandchildren of Vikings had more in common with their current neighbors than their Viking ancestors.

CENTRALIZED POWER

As Viking leaders gained power, they brought more people and communities under their control. Accepting a king's rule offered advantages, such as greater safety and security. Over time the kings of Denmark, Norway, and Sweden became more interested in building political power than in plunder. They reined in the raiding that had once characterized Viking life.

monastery —a building where monks live and work

CHRISTIANITY

Some Viking leaders converted to Christianity as a way to gain power. In the late 900s, the kings of Denmark, Norway, and Sweden all converted. They encouraged or forced their people to follow suit. Having a common faith contributed to a sense of national identity. Also, sharing the faith with other European powers reduced tensions. War was still common, but Christianity's more peaceful teachings helped curb the bloodthirsty Viking traditions. It also eventually led to the end of the Viking practice of slavery.

FACT

The Norman Conquest of England in 1066 is usually considered the end of the Viking Age.

William the Conqueror rides into London in triumph in 1066.

LASTING VIKING LORE

For centuries Viking knowledge and tales were passed along by storytellers. Listeners gathered around poets to enjoy their stories about gods, heroes, legends, and histories. Here are a few examples of tales and knowledge kept alive by Viking storytellers.

Poetic Edda

These 34 poems feature Old Norse mythology and legends. They include *Voluspá*, or "The Prophecy of the Seeress." It tells the Norse myth of how the world was created. It also contains *Ragnarök*, a tale of how the world ends. The *Poetic Edda* also offers wise sayings and tips about living an honorable life. Here is an example about keeping a good friend:

Know this, if you have a friend
whom you trust well,
go to visit him often,
for the path which no-one treads
grows with underbrush
and high grass.

the god Thor dressed up as the goddess Freyja

Thrymskvida

This favorite Norse myth is also included in the *Poetic Edda*. The giant Thrymr steals Thor's powerful hammer Mjöllnir. As ransom for the weapon, Thrymr demands marriage to the beautiful goddess Freyja. Instead, the trickster Loki dresses up Thor in a wedding dress. Loki goes along, disguised as a bridesmaid. Thor eats an entire ox at the wedding feast and displays other crude, amusing behavior while pretending to be Freyja. When Mjöllnir is given to him as part of the wedding ceremony, Thor throws off his disguise. He uses his hammer to slay Thrymr and the other giants.

Heimskringla

This collection of sagas tracks the adventures of Norway's kings. It begins with the myth of how the Norwegian kings descended from the god Odin. The middle part follows the career of king Olaf Haraldsson. It tells of his days as a young warrior, his seizure of the kingdom, and his efforts to force his subjects to adopt Christianity. The *Heimskringla* is filled with legends, but also gives some truthful historical accounts. One historical account is the story of King Harald Hardrada's invasion of England in 1066.

Loki is tortured in a scene from the Ragnarök called "The Doom of the Gods."

TRACES OF VIKINGS TODAY

Viking history and symbols continue to capture people's imaginations.

- Many parts of the British and American legal systems have roots in Norse law, including trial by jury. Even the word *law* is a Norse term. An outlaw was a convicted person forced to leave the village for breaking the law.
- More than a thousand years ago, the Althing was a big public gathering to decide important political matters in Iceland. Today that country's national assembly is still called the Althing.
- The Mighty Thor is a popular comic book hero.
- Decorating evergreen trees for Christmas has roots with the pagan Norse. They hung pieces of food, clothing, and small statues of their gods on trees as part of midwinter festivals.
- The Viking is a popular mascot for sports teams, including the Minnesota Vikings of the National Football League.
- In 1974 the National Aeronautics and Space Administration (NASA) launched the Viking probe to explore Mars. This took place on the 1,100-year anniversary of the first settlement of Iceland.
- The *Hobbit* and *The Lord of the Rings* by J.R.R. Tolkien get much of their inspiration from Viking themes and folklore.
- Richard Wagner's famous opera, *The Ring of the Nibelung*, is based on Viking mythology.
- Viking invaders carried many common words to England where they took root in the English language. These include anger, berserk, keel, lift, ransack, rock, sister, snub, stagger, and weak.
- Four days of the week are named after Norse gods. Tuesday is named for Tyr, the god of war. Wednesday is named for Odin, who is sometimes called Woden and Wotan. Thursday honors Thor. Friday is named for the goddess Freya.

Viking probe

Minnesota Vikings

Glossary

abbey (AB-ee)—a place where monks live and work that is led by an abbot

Anglo-Saxon (ANG-lo SAK-suhn)—a person who settled in England in the fifth and sixth centuries A.D.

archaeologist (ar-kee-OL-uh-jist)—someone who studies ancient buildings and artifacts to learn about the past

artifact (ART-uh-fakt)—an object made and used by humans in the past

artisan (AR-tuh-zuhn)—someone who is skilled at making something

barbarian (bahr-BAIR-ee-uhn)—someone who is wild and uncivilized

colonize (KOL-uh-nyze)—to settle a new area

draft (DRAFT)—a measurement of how deep a boat sinks into the water

mercenary (MUR-suh-nayr-ee)—a soldier who is paid to fight for a foreign army

monastery (MON-uh-ster-ee)—a building where monks live and work

Norse (NORSS)—relating to Scandinavia or Scandinavian people

pagan (PAY-guhn)—someone who is not a member of the Christian, Jewish, or Muslim religions; a pagan may worship many gods or follow no religion

tribute (TRIB-yoot)—something given as a sign of respect and admiration

Read More

Adams, Simon. *The Kingfisher Atlas of the Medieval World.* Boston, Mass.: Kingfisher, 2007.

Lassieur, Allison. *Life as a Viking: an Interactive History Adventure.* You Choose Books. Mankato, Minn.: Capstone Press, 2011.

Margeson, Susan. *Viking.* DK Eyewitness Books. New York: Dorling Kindersley , 2010.

Internet sites

FactHound offers a safe, fun way to find Internet sites related to this book. All of the sites on FactHound have been researched by our staff.

Here's all you do:

Visit *www.facthound.com*

Type in this code: 9781429666039

Index